LOST WORLDS

KINGFISHER
LONDON & NEW YORK

Copyright © 2009 by Kingfisher
Text and artwork copyright © 2009 by John Howe

Published in the United States by Kingfisher,
175 Fifth Ave., New York, NY 10010
Kingfisher is an imprint of Macmillan Children's Books, London.

Distributed in the U.S. by Macmillan, 175 Fifth Ave., New York, NY 10010
Distributed in Canada by H.B. Fenn and Company Ltd., 34 Nixon Road, Bolton, Ontario L7E 1W2

Library of Congress Cataloging-in-Publication data has been applied for.

ISBN: 978-0-7534-6107-5

Kingfisher books are available for special promotions and premiums. For details contact:
Special Markets Department, Macmillan, 175 Fifth Avenue, New York, NY 10010.

For more information, please visit www.kingfisherpublications.com

Printed in China
3 5 7 9 8 6 4 2
2TR/0110/LFG/SCHOY/157MA/C

LOST WORLDS

BY JOHN HOWE

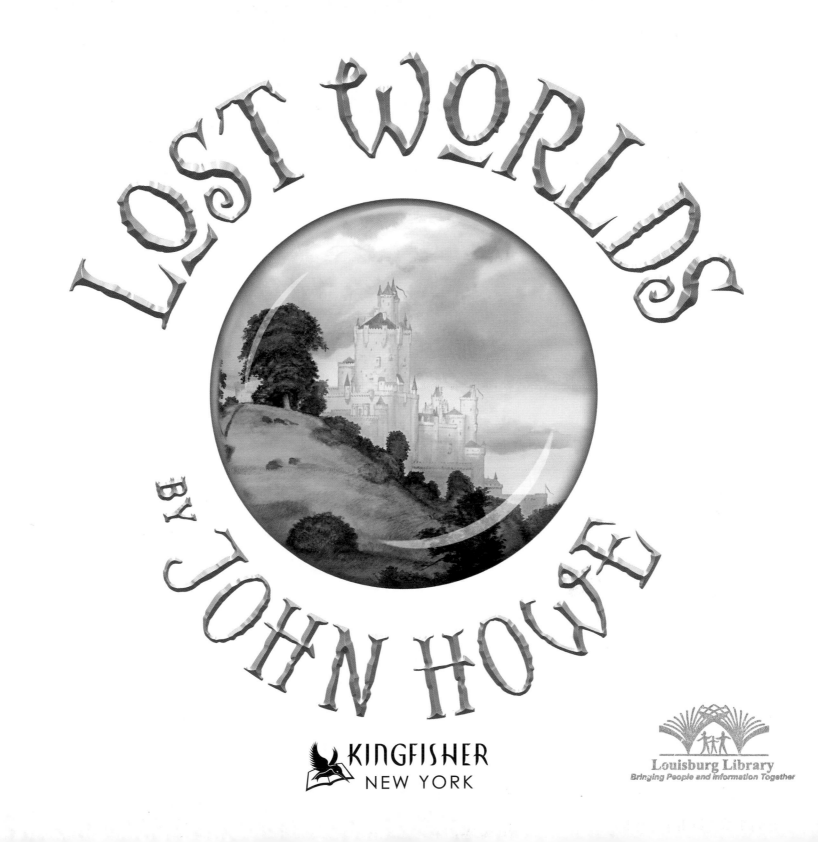

KINGFISHER
NEW YORK

Contents

John Howe's illustrations of *The Lord of the Rings* are beloved by J. R. R. Tolkien's readers and, with Alan Lee's work, were the basis of the film trilogy's imagery. In devising the on-screen look for Gandalf, both Gray and White, we had John's version to measure up to. After all, the books' old wizard with "bushy eyebrows that stuck out beyond the brim of his hat" would have looked ridiculous on screen. So when enthusiasts praised me for being "exactly as I'd always imagined Gandalf to be," they were surely remembering John Howe's pictures rather than Tolkien's text.

It's the same with the pictures in this unique book. Worlds are imagined and illustrated, becoming real in front of our eyes. Not that John is some conjurer of cheap tricks. His magic has a purpose: to make us think and wonder about distant places and people in times gone by. It's impossible to gaze at his wide yet detailed landscapes and not feel uplifted. The sensation reminds me of the first time I flew as a child, low over the ground, and saw the world afresh. *Lost Worlds* goes further than an airplane can, without our leaving the armchair. Like flying in our dreams, here we can oversee Atlantis and Camelot and believe again in unicorns. This is a book for all ages, to stimulate the child in us and fulfill our adult fantasies. At the same time, there is a modesty in John's text, as if he had simply had an idea that amused him and generously wanted us to share it. The whole enterprise seems effortless, a measure of its artistry.

I, for one, am again in his debt.

Ian McKellen

Sir Ian McKellen,
actor, Gandalf in *The Lord of the Rings*

Hunting for Unicorns — a Word from John Howe

Alicorns, or unicorn's horns, were once considered antidotes for poison. Kings, princes, royal ambassadors, and popes might carry a piece of alicorn with them on their travels, just in case they fell ill. The horns were worth ten times their weight in gold. But where did the idea of unicorns come from? How do we know what they looked like? How can we explain the astonishing popularity of creatures that never existed? Like all history, there is never just one answer. Mentioned seven times in the Bible, unicorns were among the creatures in the Garden of Eden. They were said to inhabit Prester John's kingdom. But the creatures remained elusive, although surely they existed—if not, where did the horns come from?

Holding a narwhal tooth, still wishing unicorns might exist.

Only one living creature, the narwhal, possesses a long, spiral "horn," but it is actually a tooth. But, of course, the people who braved the North Atlantic Ocean wouldn't reveal where they had obtained their lucrative prizes, which were sold as unicorn horns for great riches to kings, popes, and princes. Searching the past is like hunting for unicorns. The idea of this unique animal filled a space in imaginations, and it came to symbolize many things. Unicorns may never have existed, but they certainly needed to. Fancy and fact—tall tales and very real horns—combined over centuries to create an astonishing myth. We need unicorns.

In much the same way, we need history. The world is a big place, and its past is even bigger —and it is full of worlds that have been lost. What is a world, and how do you lose one? If history is any indication, humanity has created worlds from the very beginning, both by building hearths and by gazing at the stars in wonder. New worlds replace old; knowledge is gained and lost. A new world is born with each person, and one dies with each. Your world is not the same as mine, and though we may share much in common, each world is unique.

How do we know that facts are really true? History is not necessarily what happened but more often what someone said happened. Wherever possible, I have tried to choose the most plausible of the various facts. Wrong, right (or somewhere in between), they are the choices that appeared best to me. History is about picking up the pieces, whether they are dug out of the ground or discovered in old letters and stories. And, especially, history is about trying to put the pieces together, although each piece is from a different puzzle.

There are two kinds of lost worlds: those abandoned in time, buried and forgotten, like Aratta or Mohenjo-Daro, and the ones that live in the imagination, from Atlantis to Camelot. The first ones we might call real, since they once had streets filled with people. The latter are real, too, but in a different way; they embody our need for symbols and meaning. Each world tells us where we have come from, physically and spiritually. Some worlds are both.

Worlds can be lost because, in order to exist, they must not be found. Invisible, sunken in the ocean's depths, perched on inaccessible peaks, or buried in the center of the earth, they are beyond our grasp. Because they are out of reach, they remain the kingdoms of those who claim to have seen them—marvelous places for a lucky few. Naturally, they must remain hidden or they would lose their magic and appeal. They have no place in our world but symbolize our yearning for those imagined places where everything is perfect. In the same way, lost civilizations become stories handed down in legend, or artifacts that emerge from careful digging in the past. Either way, they are ultimately beyond our grasp. Like the unicorn.

This book is not written to give definitive answers; it is written to tell stories, the fascinating stories that make up our past, real or imagined. It is written to offer a modest door that opens on to the worlds themselves. What we make of the past, and what it may tell us about ourselves, is a never-ending story, of which this book is one minuscule chapter in a multitude. I hope it will encourage you to read on.

John Howe

9

The Garden of Eden

Eastward in Eden, God made a garden. It was beautiful and bountiful, with every type of tree pleasant to look at and bearing fruit to eat. Two trees were very special: the Tree of Knowledge of Good and Evil and the Tree of Life. The serpent tempted Eve, and she and Adam both tasted forbidden fruit from the Tree of Knowledge.

God, fearing Adam and Eve might eat from the other tree, the Tree of Life, and thus become immortal, cast them out of the garden. To the serpent God said, "Upon thy belly shalt thou go, and dust shalt thou eat all the days of thy life." Under the stern gaze of the cherubim, Adam and Eve left the beautiful garden and were barred from returning by a flashing sword of flame. According to Genesis, the first book of the Bible, this is how humanity set out on its long journey into the wilderness.

In the Bible, the garden is situated in the east of the land called Eden. *Eden* is a Hebrew word meaning "delight," derived from *Edin*, a Sumerian word meaning "fertile plain." The origin of the word is probably Ubaidian. The Ubaidian culture was a prehistoric Mesopotamian civilization that thrived between 5500 and 4000 B.C.

When Adam and Eve were expelled from the garden, winged cherubim with flaming swords stood guard. They could never return to Eden.

God created all the beasts and birds of the earth and placed them in the garden. God gave Adam dominion over all the other creatures.

In one biblical legend, the unicorn was the first animal Adam named. Unwilling to come aboard Noah's Ark, the unicorns perished in the Great Flood.

According to Jewish tradition, the Garden of Eden and Paradise are one and the same. Islamic tradition places Eden in heaven, where it is one of four heavenly gardens. The 17th-century philosopher Baruch Spinoza (1632–1677), founder of modern biblical criticism, stated that the garden was destroyed in the Great Flood that God sent to destroy the world.

Archaeologists generally agree that the garden was situated somewhere in the plains of Mesopotamia. The climate in the region underwent a severe change 8,000 years ago, which may explain the notion of people leaving a fertile garden for harsher lands. More recently, a British archaeologist claimed to have located Eden in the valley formed by an extinct volcano in northwestern Iran.

Mongolia, India, Ethiopia, and Turkey have also been thoroughly searched by biblical scholars. Less likely locations—Java, Sri Lanka, the Seychelles, Brabant, Florida, and Bristol, England—have also been seriously

proposed. The Mormons, following a revelation of the church founder Joseph Smith, situate the Garden of Eden at Independence, Missouri.

It is as difficult to dismiss the Garden of Eden as pure fantasy as it is to take it literally—passionate debates have been going on since the Bible was written. However, as a story it is particularly rich and meaningful—Adam and Eve's flight from the garden places us firmly on the road of discovery shared by all.

According to the Bible, the garden is watered by a river that flows from Eden. This river separates into four more rivers, called Pison, Gihon, Hiddekel, and Euphrates.

14

Babylon

Said to be a gift from King Nebuchadnezzar II to his wife, Amytis of Media, the Hanging Gardens of Babylon were one of the Seven Wonders of the World. The Babylonians learned how to control the flooding of the mighty Tigris and Euphrates rivers, and they practiced extensive irrigation, making the Hanging Gardens of Babylon a lush, green oasis in the vast Mesopotamian city on the plains.

The Hanging Gardens of Babylon were built by King Nebuchadnezzar II around 600 B.C. According to the Greek historian Strabo, whose *Geographica* was published in 7 B.C., "The garden is quadrangular in shape . . . It consists of arched vaults, which are situated, one after another, on checkered, cubelike foundations . . . The ascent to the uppermost terrace-roofs is made by a stairway; and alongside these stairs there were screws, through which the water was continually conducted up into the garden from the Euphrates by those appointed for this purpose."

Babylon was one of the greatest cities of its time. The name comes from the Akkadian *babilan*, meaning "the Gate of the Gods." Founded in the 24th century B.C. by Sargon of Akkad, the city was built on the banks of the Euphrates River, one half on each side. By 1700 B.C., it was probably the largest city in the world.

This map of Mesopotamia is from c. 700–500 B.C. Babylon is in the center of the circle, which is surrounded by a body of water called the "Sea of Salt."

Babylon's buildings were made principally of mud bricks. They were molded and glazed in bright colors and depicted bulls, lions, dragons, and other creatures and beings, including the god Marduk.

The gardens of Babylon were watered via a system of screws, which were turned to distribute the water to different terraces.

Conquered by the Assyrians in 698 B.C., Babylon's walls, temples, and palaces were razed. The Babylonians overthrew Assyrian rule in 626, and the new king, Nebuchadnezzar II, rebuilt the city, creating a new Babylon that was said to be even more splendid than the old one. According to the Greek historian Herodotus (c. 484–c. 425 B.C.), Babylon was square with an outer wall almost 14 mi. (23km) long and with eight gates, including the famous Ishtar Gate.

In 539 B.C., the Persian king Cyrus the Great conquered Babylon. Unable to breach the walls, Cyrus's troops diverted water from the Euphrates. When water levels dropped, the troops marched into the city through the river gates, where the Euphrates entered and exited the city. Cyrus released the Jews, allowing them to return to Jerusalem. Babylon then became the capital of the Persian Empire.

Two centuries later, in 331 B.C., Alexander the Great conquered Babylon. But after his death in 323 B.C., his empire was divided among his generals, and fighting engulfed the region once more.

By 141 B.C., when Babylon became a province of the Parthian Empire (remaining under Persian rule until A.D. 650), the once great city, home to one of the Seven Wonders of the World, was a desolate and abandoned ruin.

The gardens were destroyed in an earthquake around the first century B.C. Some scholars believe that they never existed.

About 85 mi. (137km) south of present-day Baghdad, Iraq, on the banks of the Euphrates River, a low hill, or "tell," of broken mud-brick buildings and debris covering 12 sq. mi. (30km²) is all that remains of the once glorious city.

The Tower of Babel by Pieter Breughel the Elder, painted in 1563. The tower was a popular theme among painters of the Renaissance. The seven-story building was completed in 600 B.C. and measured 300 ft. (91m) high.

17

Thebes

Dawn rises over the Nile Valley, the sun mirrored on the wide, slow water of the sacred river. It outlines two colossal statues, one broken at the waist, its torso and head lying in a pile of rubble at its base, the other intact, although damaged by sand and wind. A dozen travelers lounge around, their guides quieting restless donkeys and camels. A shepherd drives his flock before him, heading for higher ground; the Nile in flood has left shallow lakes at the statues' feet. Almost imperceptibly, a fine, keening whistle is heard, increasing in volume as the sun warms the mountains behind Thebes, the Seat of Kings. The colossi of Memnon are singing for Eos, the goddess of the dawn.

With the Rosetta Stone, found in Thebes, the Egyptian hieroglyphs were finally deciphered.

The Greeks and Romans were the first foreign tourists to visit the colossi. The figures were thought to represent Memnon, the legendary son of Eos. An earthquake shook the region in 27 B.C., breaking the northernmost statue in half. More than two centuries later, in A.D. 199, the Roman emperor Septimus Severus repaired the fallen statue, clumsily mending it with sandstone blocks. Reassembled, the statue became mute.

The colossi of Memnon were sculpted to flank the door of the even more colossal mortuary temple of Amenhotep III. From Thebes (today's Luxor), Amenhotep III ruled Egypt from 1386 to 1349 B.C. Thebes was in fact two cities, a city of the living on the east bank of the Nile River and a city of the dead on the west bank. When the pharaohs gave up constructing their pyramid tombs, they chose a site near Thebes dominated by a pyramid-shaped mountain. This burial ground is known as the Valley of the Kings.

The origins of Thebes are unknown. In 2134 B.C., Egypt was split into two kingdoms, ruled by Thebes in the south and Memphis in the north. The land was reunited under Mentuhotep I, who made Thebes the capital. From 1550 to 1069 B.C., it was the greatest city in Egypt. When Thutmosis I died in 1492 B.C., he became the first pharaoh to be buried in the necropolis of the Valley of the Kings.

In 1386 B.C., Amenhotep III became pharaoh, and he spent his energy on building great monuments. His mortuary temple at Thebes was one of the grandest buildings ever constructed, but erosion from the Nile in flood may have undermined its sandy foundations. In less than two centuries it was a ruin. Succeeding pharaohs pillaged the stones to construct their own monuments. Soon little was left except for the two massive statues.

Some of the greatest surviving paintings from ancient Egypt were unearthed from Thebes. This tomb painting was colored with soot for black areas, desert stones for tones of red, yellow, and white, and ground glass for blue and green colors.

20

The statues well merit the name "colossi"—each one, carved from a single block of quartzite, was 52 ft. (16m) high and 20 ft. (6.1m) wide and weighed several hundred tons. They were to be the silent witnesses of Thebes's destiny.

In 664 B.C., Thebes became one of many cities plundered by the Assyrians. Then the Persians arrived in 525 B.C. and again in 343 B.C., followed 11 years later by Alexander the Great. Finally, Thebes was destroyed by the Romans in 30 B.C. and practically abandoned by the A.D. first century.

In July 1798, when the French general Napoleon Bonaparte (1769–1821) invaded Egypt, he brought a team of scientists with his army. They explored ruins, dug up artifacts, and made maps and drawings. Modern Egyptology was in the making.

Today, international teams of archaeologists are still at work uncovering Egypt's rich and varied past. Many sites are open to the public, but dozens more are closed to preserve them. It is no longer legal to dig up artifacts and ship them for sale abroad. Tourists still come from all over the world to admire the colossi of Memnon.

Between the temples of Luxor and Karnak, Amenhotep III laid out beautiful gardens, with an avenue lined with ram-headed sphinxes carved in stone, each with a statue of the pharaoh between its paws.

Napoleon's troops considered the colossi of Memnon excellent objects for target practice, and the faces of the statues were irreparably damaged.

Atlantis

Gradually, the Atlanteans fell from grace, fighting among themselves, as each successive generation abandoned divine ideals for petty quarrels. They no longer admired beauty for its own sake but preferred to hoard precious stones and metals. This angered Zeus, who chastised his brother Poseidon. In sorrow and anger, Poseidon raised the sea, and a great wave engulfed Atlantis. This cataclysm took place, Plato said, 9,000 years before his time.

The city that grew around the mountain's foot was vast and opulent. Ships entered the harbors through high, vaulted tunnels. Atlantis was girded with stout walls and towers made of red, black, and white stone.

Plato (c. 428 B.C.–c. 347 B.C.) claims to have taken his story of Atlantis from an account written by a fellow Greek, Solon (638–558 B.C.), who heard the tale from the priests of Neith in Egypt. The story goes that Atlantis was made by the Greek god Poseidon for a beautiful woman named Kleito. Poseidon shaped a grand island 430 mi. (700km) across, with rich forests and fertile plains.

Near the southern coast, Poseidon carved a mountaintop into a palace for Kleito and enclosed it with three circular moats. The imperial palace was covered in silver, with pinnacles of gold. Next to it stood the temple of Poseidon. "In the interior of the temple the roof was of ivory, curiously wrought everywhere with gold and silver and orichalcum [an unknown metal more precious than gold] . . ."

It seems that Plato's tale made little impression on his contemporaries, and the story itself slowly sank into oblivion. But Atlantis was not destined to remain forever beneath the waves. Several centuries later, Pliny the Elder (A.D. 23–79) cautiously confirmed that Atlantis must indeed have been beyond the Pillars of Hercules, adding "if we are to believe Plato." It was not until scholars rediscovered Plato's writings in the 15th century that minds turned once more to Atlantis. Geographers happily placed it in yet-uncharted oceans, along with other isles from fable.

This 1664 map by German geographer Athanasius Kircher places his "Insula Atlantis" in the middle of the Atlantic Ocean, between Africa and the Americas.

In 1553, Spanish historian Francesco López de Gómara (c. 1511–c. 1566) suggested that the New World (America) and Atlantis were one and the same. However, Atlantis gradually disappeared from the ever-changing maps of the Age of Discovery. It was not until 1870, when a retired lawyer named Ignatius T. T. Donnelly wrote *Atlantis, the Antediluvian World*, that the sunken city finally reemerged with a flourish. Donnelly's book was an instant bestseller. Suddenly, Atlantis was everywhere. It was said to be the cradle of civilization—all ancient cultures (the Egyptians, the Babylonians, the Aztecs, the Maya) were pale copies of Atlantis and had been founded by survivors of the catastrophe.

Atlantis was also identified with the mythical continent of Mu in the Pacific. Other geographical candidates were enthusiastically proposed: Atlantis was said to be off the coast of Africa, in Algeria, the Caucasus, the Caspian Sea, Spitzbergen, Malta, Brazil, Iceland, India, and the British Isles, among other places. Even the moon has been suggested.

So, exalted rewriting of history and geography aside, where and what was Atlantis? If only we could ask Plato himself, the riddle might be solved, but we must make do with the few clues we have.

If such a grand island had indeed sunk, geology should show some trace. But although ridges and mountains abound in the middle Atlantic, they are the result of the pushing and grinding of the surface of our planet, not of sinking continents. The bed of the Mediterranean Sea has revealed no sunken cities.

The most likely explanation is that Plato, impatient with the pettiness of his fellow Athenians, never intended his story to be more than an elaborate morality tale of a people who go astray and are thus punished by the god that created them. In the end, Plato has the first and last word. Atlantis is beyond our reach, beyond our most wishful thinking, over the horizon in the realm of the imagination, under the restless waves of myth and legend.

These Minoan wrestlers are painted on a wall in Thera (now Santorini). A volcano erupted at Thera, possibly destroying the Minoan civilization on neighboring Crete. This cataclysmic event may have captured Plato's imagination generations later.

Knossos

Theseus gripped the hilt of
his sword with both hands,
flattening himself against
the damp wall, trying to remain still.
He had spent hours making his
way to the heart of the Labyrinth.
The Minotaur was very near—
he could hear the creature
breathing, like an angry
bull about to charge.

This tablet from Knossos has a script named "Linear A" by Arthur Evans.

The legend of the Minotaur was well known to the ancient Greeks. According to Greek history, in the fifth century B.C. the creation of the world was followed by an age of great deeds of men such as Theseus.

Crete's first queen, Europa, had three sons, Minos, Rhadamanthus, and Sarpedon, who fought one another for the throne. Minos prayed to the sea god, Poseidon, for a white bull to sacrifice to help him win the fight. A beautiful white bull arose from the sea and Minos defeated his brothers. But he kept the creature alive, thinking Poseidon would not notice. The angry god made Minos's wife, Pasiphaë, fall in love with the bull, and she gave birth to a huge, bull-headed monster—the Minotaur. Minos commanded his architect, Daedalus, to create a gigantic Labyrinth next to

A storage vessel known as a pithos stands in the palace of Minos at Knossos, Crete. These containers were often as tall as a man and were used to store grain, oil, and wine. They would have been made entirely by hand.

the palace at Knossos, where he locked the creature away. Many years later, Androgeus, the son of Minos, was killed by the Athenians. To avenge the murder, Minos conquered Athens and demanded that seven Athenian youths and seven maidens be sent every ninth year to Crete. They had to enter the Labyrinth—there to be devoured by the Minotaur. Theseus, the son of Aegeus, ruler of Athens, offered to slay the monster. When Theseus arrived at Knossos, Ariadne, Minos's daughter, fell in love with him and secretly gave him a ball of thread, which would enable him to retrace his steps in the Labyrinth. With Aegeus's sword, Theseus killed the Minotaur and escaped.

To the Greeks, these events were seen both as history and story, but the passing of time changed them into legends. Thousands of years later, the Labyrinth and the land of Minos reemerged, along with the vanished culture that created them, out of the ground itself. In the 19th century, scholars were rereading the *Iliad*

Arthur Evans did more than unearth and preserve the ruins of Knossos—he set out to rebuild Minos's palace. He even hired a Swiss painter to reconstruct the damaged frescoes.

Sir Arthur Evans with a bull's head rhyton (drinking horn) and a stone seal (below), both found at Knossos.

Enraged by the Minotaur's death, Minos imprisoned Daedalus and his son, Icarus, in a high tower. They collected bird feathers and made wings to escape. But Icarus flew too high, falling to his death when the sun melted the wax holding his wings together.

and other Greek classics and pondering just where the events had taken place. A British aristocrat, Arthur Evans (1851–1941), went on the trail of the Minotaur. Evans was intrigued by a collection of mysterious engraved stone seals that came, he was told, from Crete. He thought the marks on the seals may have represented a form of writing far older than Phoenician, the earliest known writing in the Mediterranean. Evans was convinced that an as-yet-unknown civilization had preceded the seals, and that the secret was to be found in Knossos.

In 1900, Evans began his 30-year excavation of Knossos. Little by little, the walls of a vast palace emerged, along with a road, a smaller palace, and a burial ground. Evans realized that his intuition was right. While he had expected to find a center of Mycenean (early Greek) culture, he in fact discovered an older, unknown civilization from Crete itself. Evans called it Minoan, in honor of Minos.

In the 15th century B.C., Knossos was destroyed. For many years it was believed that the powerful eruption of the volcano Thera—now Santorini, 68 mi. (109km) north of Crete—created a tidal wave that engulfed Knossos and wiped out the Minoan civilization. Such a dramatic end to a lost world appealed to scholars of Evans's time, and it made Knossos a possible candidate for the long-lost city of Atlantis. Historians now believe that while the eruption of Thera did not destroy Minoan civilization, it may have disrupted and weakened it to such an extent that the Myceneans were able to invade and conquer them.

Troy

The wheels of the huge wooden
Thorse rumbled as the joyful Trojans
hauled it through the city gates.
After ten interminable years, the siege
had ended. The Greeks had gone, leaving
only this tribute to Trojan bravery. But
Laocoön, priest of Poseidon, cried out in
warning, "Bring this thing inside our walls,
you will bring doom with it!" He flung a
spear at the wooden horse. It thudded into
the planking and stuck there, quivering.

31

Later that night, as the Trojans slept, the Greek soldiers crept out of their hiding place inside the wooden horse. They silently opened the gate to the city where the Greek army was waiting outside. The troops marched into Troy and set fire to the city.

A replica of a jewelry pin from Priam's treasure, Troy.

Thousands of years later in Germany in 1830, a wide-eyed eight-year-old named Heinrich Schliemann held his breath as his father recounted, for the umpteenth time, the *Iliad*. King Priam of Troy, his beautiful daughter Helen, the hero Achilles, the Trojan Horse, and a thousand ships filled his mind with wonder. "Did Troy really exist?" he asked. "Perhaps," replied his father, "but if ever it was real, it has long been buried and lost." Later, in the darkness of his room, his eyes closed tight, young Heinrich willed Troy to exist and vowed to one day find it. Eventually, at the age of 42, Schliemann trained his sights on one goal: he set out to find the lost city of Troy.

In the *Iliad*, the Greek poet Homer states that Troy was a "well-walled," "broad" city with "lofty gates" and "fine towers." He describes the Trojans as "horse tamers," and they were generally believed to have been excellent horsemen. Homer details the layout of the town, describing Priam's palace, a temple to Apollo, and an agora where the citizens met. He depicts Troy as a grand city, well defended by towering ramparts. But Homer does not really say where it is.

By the Middle Ages, Troy had become a legend. The kings of the Britons were traced back to the Trojan hero Aeneas. The kings of Norway were said to be descended from those of Troy. Scholars passed from marveling at the stories of Troy to wondering where it might actually have been situated. By 1820, likely spots on the Turkish coast had been designated. In 1870, Schliemann began excavations at Hisarlik in Turkey, where he uncovered ruins dating from the second or third century B.C. He kept digging.

A gold death mask, called the Mask of Agamemnon, was found by Schliemann in Mycenae. Agamemnon was the Greek hero who led the war against the Trojans.

Sophia Schliemann wearing jewelry that her husband unearthed from Troy.

A pithos that was found during Schliemann's excavations.

In 1871, Schliemann unearthed ramparts almost 7 ft. (2m) thick—he was convinced that he had discovered Priam's palace. He dug deeper, and city after city appeared. By 1873, he had found seven cities—but which one was Troy?

Then, the day before digging was to end, like the final page of a storybook tale, Schliemann made his great discovery— "Priam's treasure." This find consisted of bracelets, two gold diadems, dozens of earrings, daggers, a shield, thousands of coins, and many other items.

Historians now agree that Troy was not only a real place, but exactly where Schliemann believed it to be. The hill of Hisarlik is a "tell"—a mound made of layer upon layer of cities, each one built on top of the ruins of others. All the cities are numbered. Troy I is more than 5,000 years old, a city from the Bronze Age. Troy VIIa, the best candidate as the Troy of the *Iliad*, was built around 1300 B.C. We will never know if there actually was a Trojan Horse, but the city was clearly destroyed, perhaps by war, in 1180 B.C.

A Trojan earring found by Schliemann in Troy II.

A thousand Greek ships arrived at the walls of Troy to rescue Helen, who had been abducted by Paris, the son of Priam. The ensuing Trojan War would last ten bitter years.

Those who angered the gods were
cruelly punished. Prometheus, who stole
fire from Zeus and gave it to humankind, was
chained to a crag on Mount Kaukasos. Every day at
dawn, Zeus's great eagle swooped to tear Prometheus's
flesh. Prometheus remained for generations on his lofty crag,
until he was at last set free by the hero Herakles (Hercules).

Mount Olympus

The Olympian gods chose a mountaintop dwelling place well above the world of humans, placing stone walls all around the summit. A gateway of clouds shielded their gleaming palaces and temples from mortal eyes. From there, they could survey (and often meddle in) mortal affairs in the world below.

The original 12 Olympian (Greek) gods are known as the Dodekatheon. Zeus rules the heavens, his brother Poseidon rules the sea, and another brother, Hades, rules the realm of the dead. The Horae, goddesses of the seasons, guard the cloud-gate of Olympus. The walls and palaces were built by the Cyclopes, whom Zeus freed from Tartarus, a gloomy pit in Hades' realm where they were imprisoned. In gratitude, they toiled mightily to build the walls and gave Zeus the thunderbolts he throws in anger.

Zeus holds court seated on a throne of polished black marble atop a dais of seven steps, each one a different color of the rainbow. The topmost step is enameled cerulean blue, symbolizing the sky, which belongs to Zeus alone. A golden eagle with ruby eyes perches on the right arm of the throne. Zeus's wife, Hera, sits next to him on a throne of ivory with three steps leading up.

The gilded marble palace of Zeus and Hera overlooks the cities of Athens, Thebes, Sparta, Corinth, Argos, and Mycenae to the south. It has a beautiful garden with a clear pool reflecting the sky. The remaining gods and goddesses live on each side of the square court in the center of Olympus. Lesser gods dwell in small houses. There is even a menagerie, where the gods keep their sacred animals. To the north are the kitchen, banquet hall, armory, workshops, servants' quarters, and stables.

There are many mountains in Greece and Turkey that bear the name Mount Olympus, but the highest one in Greece naturally came to be seen as the home of the gods. Mount Olympus is 9,577 ft. (2,919m) high, though no one, of course, has ever seen the gods there.

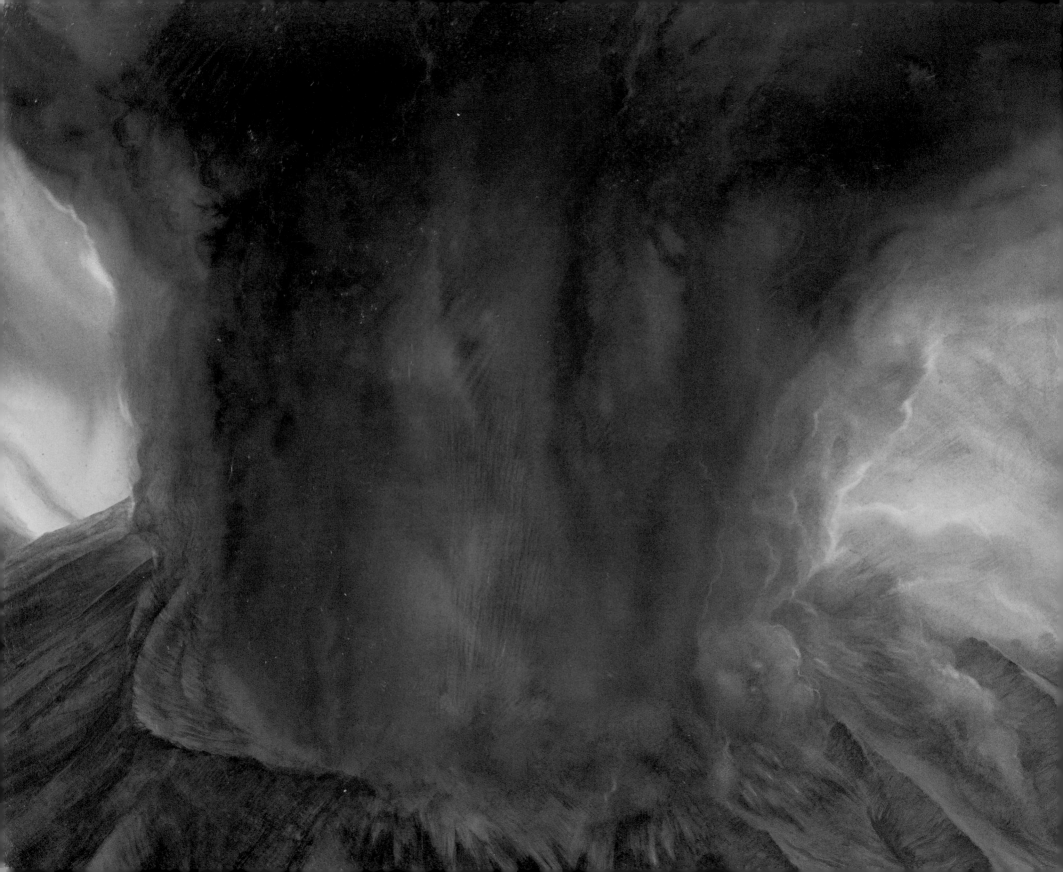

Pompeii

Just after 1 A.M. on August 24, A.D. 79, the eruption begins. A column of smoke and ash rises more than 12 mi. (19km) into the sky. In the preceding days, signs had told of the coming disaster. Several small earthquakes had shaken the region, wells had dried up, and springs had stopped flowing. Dogs had howled, and birds had been strangely silent. This was not the first time Vesuvius had erupted. Already eruptions in 900 B.C. and again in 320 B.C. had covered the region in dust and ash, blowing the top off the mountain. But for four centuries the volcano had been asleep.

The first city on the site of Pompeii was built between the eighth and sixth centuries B.C. by the Oscians from central Italy. Captured first by the Etruscans, the city was then occupied by the Greeks between 525 and 475 B.C. In 80 B.C., the town became a Roman colony, which rapidly grew to be an important seaport for goods destined for Rome. By A.D. 79, Pompeii was a thriving metropolis of some 20,000 inhabitants. Then the world exploded.

This two-headed snake bracelet was found in the ruins of Pompeii.

"A cloud, from which mountain was uncertain at this distance, was ascending, the appearance of which I cannot give you a more exact description of than by likening it to that of a pine tree, for it shot up to a great height in the form of a very tall trunk, which spread itself out at the top into a sort of branches." So wrote Pliny the Younger after witnessing the eruption.

Mount Vesuvius sits atop a faultline, a place where the plates that compose the earth's crust rub against each other. The slowly grinding plates created enormous pressure under the volcano, and the lava plug that sealed the mouth of Vesuvius finally cracked, shooting thousands of tons of dust and ash skyward.

Severe earthquakes in A.D. 62 and 64 toppled statues and collapsed houses. Emperor Nero wondered if the city should be abandoned, but stubbornly the Pompeiians rebuilt, ignoring the warning. Many buildings were still being repaired when Vesuvius erupted 15 years later.

Stones and ash rained down on Pompeii. Buildings caved in under the weight of the ash, and the cloud and smoke blocked out the sun. Eighteen hours after the eruption began, a pyroclastic flow (a dense liquid of very hot ash and lava) poured downhill at great speed. By the time it reached the northern walls of Pompeii, most of the population had fled.

One of the most famous plaster models taken from Pompeii is a dog with his collar, chained and unable to escape the eruption.

A dog mosaic from a house in Pompeii.

Early in the morning of August 25, a second pyroclastic surge overwhelmed Pompeii, killing those left in the city. An hour later, another surge reached Pompeii, followed shortly by a final surge of steam and mud. Pliny the Younger fled from his villa in Misenium, several miles beyond Pompeii, into the countryside. By the next morning, it was over. Pompeii had been obliterated.

Little by little, houses, farms, and vineyards covered the once more fertile region, and Pompeii was forgotten. Only in 1860 did archaeologists start work on the Pompeii site. They discovered curious holes and cavities in the ruins. They are all that remains of the unfortunate inhabitants of Pompeii. Encased in a rock-hard coating of ash, all but the skeletons have decomposed, leaving their imprints as hollows in the earth. Models were made by carefully filling the hollows with plaster.

Since 1631, 20 more eruptions have followed, mostly of smoke and ash, before the last in March 1944 destroyed the neighboring villages of San Sebastiano al Vesuvio and Massa di Somma. The years following represent the longest period of calm that Vesuvius has displayed in over 500 years.

A statue from Pompeii of the god Dionysus-Sabazius.

The Roman emperor Titus came to see the damage. Survivors wandered over the buried city, trying to find the remains of their homes. Only a few of the taller buildings emerged from a landscape of dust and ash.

The ruins of Pompeii are near the modern town of the same name. Colorful mosaics adorn walls of houses, which are reached by long, paved streets.

39

Ultima Thule

In 325 B.C., Greek navigator and geographer Pytheas sailed around Great Britain, visited the Outer Hebrides, and perhaps even ventured to Scandinavia and Iceland. Pytheas is known for recording a tale that continues to intrigue us today: the legend of Ultima Thule.

North of Britain, Pytheas claimed, lies a land called Thule: "six days' sail north from the Isles of the Pretani [Britain]" and "one day's sail from where the sea freezes." He was shown a place where the sun went to rest and noted that the day was only two or three hours long. He described Thule as "an agricultural country producing honey whose inhabitants ate fruit and milk and made a drink of grain and honey."

Two centuries later, Greek geographer Strabo wrote: "Pytheas also speaks of the waters around Thule and of those places where land properly speaking no longer exists, nor sea nor air, but a mixture of these things, like a 'marine lung,' [on] which one can neither walk nor sail." The term *marine lung* means "jellyfish"; Pytheas may have been referring to thick fog or perhaps to slush (ice, or ice that has not yet fully hardened into ice floes). Strabo also calls Pytheas a liar, claiming he invented his voyage.

When the Romans conquered Great Britain in 55 B.C., the Roman general Agricola ordered his fleet to sail around the north coast. The mysterious land of Thule, which the fleet did not reach, was seen in the distance. By the Middle Ages, Thule was a regular feature on maps, always somewhere just out of sight to the north.

The idea of Ultima Thule inspired explorers to adventure north. In A.D. 1909, American Robert E. Peary's third polar expedition reached the North Pole. The promised land of Ultima Thule was a vast and bitterly cold wilderness of ice.

Nonetheless, Thule is now on the world map, more than two millennia after Pytheas—North Greenland was formally named Thule after the mythical place.

Asgard

sgard is the sky home of the Aesir and Asynuir, the Norse gods and
goddesses. It is guarded by high walls and sturdy ramparts. Bifrost, the
rainbow bridge, links Asgard to the world of mortals. Odin, the ruler
of the gods, often crosses this bridge, riding his eight-legged horse, Sleipnir,
whose hooves sound like thunder. Odin gave one of his own eyes in exchange
for the staff he carries, cut from the living wood of Yggdrasil, the world-tree.

Yggdrasil is the ash tree that holds up the sky. It sits atop the mountain in the center
of Midgard, the world of humans. At the other side of the rainbow bridge, guarding the
entrance to Asgard, is Odin's hall, Valaskjalf. Of the many splendid halls in Asgard,
the finest is Valhalla, the Hall of the Slain. It has 540 doors, each wide enough
for 800 people to pass through together. The roof is made of golden shields.

As Christianity replaced the worship of the Norse gods in Scandinavia, the
heroes and gods of Asgard became characters of folk- and fairy tales. We also
use their names daily—as the days of the week. Tuesday is named after Tyr;
Odin (or Wotan) lends his name to Wednesday; Thursday is Thor's day; and
Friday is Frigg's day. They replaced the Roman gods, leaving Saturday
(Saturn's day), and the sun and the moon for Sunday and Monday.

Cahokia

With a bowl of smoking embers held aloft, a priest greets the rising sun. Morning over the Mississippi basin, like every morning, is a confirmation of the cosmic order of all things— the rising and setting sun, the succession of seasons, the cycle of birth, life, and death. Cahokia, with its sacred mounds and holy grounds, is the universe in miniature. A place of perfection and permanence, it is also a land of power. The sacred fire that burns atop the tallest mound—an earthen pyramid ten stories high—is never extinguished. To let it die would be akin to allowing the sun to set and never rise again.

44

In 1842, the author Charles Dickens made a trip to the United States. In his book *American Notes*, he says: "Looming in the distance . . . was another of the ancient Indian burial places, called The Monks' Mound; in memory of . . . the order of La Trappe, who founded a desolate convent there . . . when there were no settlers within a thousand miles . . ." Dickens did not realize he was contemplating the remains of what was once the largest city in the land. The terraced, rectangular pyramid of Monks Mound remained the tallest American human-made structure until 1870.

A French settlement called Cahokia had been established nearby in the early 1700s. The name refers to a tribe of Illiniwek people who were living in the area when French explorers arrived in the 1600s.

The original settlement of Cahokia began around A.D. 800, and many mounds were built. The central portion of the settlement was completely enclosed by a wooden palisade made from more than 20,000 logs. Inside were 17 mounds, of which the largest, Monks Mound, rose more than 100 ft. (30m) in four terraces. Public buildings and houses of the elite were built on the flat-topped mounds. There were plazas, residential areas, playing fields, and a series of large, circular monuments of wooden posts, called woodhenges.

Long recognized as an ancient site, it was only in the early 1900s that outraged archaeologists and politicians finally swayed public opinion in favor of preservation. It was about time—the Big Mound in Saint Louis had been razed in 1869. The rapidly expanding city had crossed the Mississippi River, and new townships surrounded the Cahokia Mounds. Today, 70 of the original 120 mounds have been preserved.

Woodhenge monuments such as this one may have served as sun calendars, to chart important dates.

Monks Mound was completed in 1150. Its summit was crowned with a large wooden temple or chief's house.

The Birdman Tablet was found on the east side of Monks Mound.

Intricate arrowheads have been found in Cahokia.

The descendants of the mound builders themselves are unknown. They left no writing to tell who they were; the only clues were dug out of the ground at the site. Little by little, the culture of the original builders has been reconstructed. Cahokian society was probably a theocracy, where priests held the power, while their rulers were believed to have descended from the sun itself.

After A.D. 800, the community grew, and by 1050, Cahokia had become a major city. By 1150, Cahokia was at the height of its power and was the largest city north of Mexico, with a population of up to 20,000.

Trade goods, such as minerals to make ornaments, came from far away to Cahokia.

By 1250, Cahokia had begun to decline, and it was deserted by 1400. No one knows what led to its being abandoned, but one explanation lies in climate change. Such a large group of people who rely on farming, hunting, and trade are at the mercy of nature—late springs, early frosts, and the extremes of drought and flooding. The cutting of trees to build houses and to feed cooking fires could have, over centuries, created erosion. Years of farming may have exhausted the land. Diseases possibly added to health problems, or perhaps external threats or internal tension broke up their society. In any case, it happened slowly, and there is no evidence of a war or disaster. We do not know what became of the Cahokians. Only the mounds remain.

Recent tests have shown that there are stone structures buried deep within Monks Mound. Cahokia is far from revealing all its mysteries.

Sports were popular in Cahokia. "Chunkey" players rolled a stone disk before them and tried to throw a long stick to the exact spot where the disk might come to a halt.

Cíbola

If gold was to be found at the end of a rainbow, the Spanish conquistadors would have unearthed it. Driven by greed for fortune and fame, they pursued dreams of cities paved with gold—dreams that became nightmares in the dripping jungles, burning deserts, and frozen mountains of the New World. No pursuit of fool's gold is more tragic than Francisco Vásquez de Coronado's fruitless quest for the Seven Cities of Cíbola.

By the end of the Middle Ages, tales of fabulous faraway lands abounded in Europe. One legend said, "In the year A.D. 713, seven bishops sailed west into the Atlantic. Somewhere beyond the horizon, they discovered the island of Antillia and founded the rich kingdom of the Seven Cities of Cíbola." However, these fabulous lands proved elusive.

In 1528, two survivors of a shipwrecked expedition in Florida, a Spaniard named Álvar Núñez Cabeza de Vaca and a slave called Esteban, brought new tales of the Cities of Gold. De Vaca wrote: "There are pearls and great riches on the coast of the South

Sea [the Pacific]."

Eleven years later, Friar Marcos de Niza set off north from Mexico City, with Esteban as a guide. Upon reaching the Sonora Valley, Esteban was sent farther north to explore. How de Niza's heart must have leapt when he received a message with a description of the golden city. He quickly followed Esteban's trail. Thirty days' march, the villagers said, would lead him to the gates of the first of the Seven Cities. However, de Niza was met instead by the news of Esteban's death and returned home without setting eyes on his goal. De Niza had tall tales to tell on his return. Cíbola, he said, was larger than Mexico City and

Preceded by four priests, Coronado led 225 mounted men, 60 foot soldiers, and a company of slaves and servants who hauled six bronze cannon. On their heels followed herds of livestock and pack animals, including 1,000 horses, 500 cattle, and 500 sheep and pigs. A rear guard comprised more than 1,300 Native Americans.

incredibly beautiful. De Niza had little evidence of Cíbola's existence, but he must have been a convincing storyteller because another expedition was launched.

On February 23, 1540, Francisco Vásquez de Coronado set out from Compostela in Mexico at the head of a grand cavalcade. After five months, the expedition arrived in Cíbola—present-day Hawikuh, New Mexico. There were no roofs of gold and no grand houses decorated with precious stones, only a collection of mud villages. Coronado sent out search parties in every direction. One explored the Grand Canyon and returned with a strange prisoner. His name was El Turco (the Turk). Yes, the Turk said, he had seen the golden cities. Far to the northeast was the fabulous kingdom of Quivira, governed by a king named Tatarrax. The royal household ate off gold plates and drank from golden cups! The Spaniards, he added, would be wise to bring many carts and wagons, lest they could not carry all the gold away.

Reluctant to return to Mexico empty-handed, Coronado set off again. He crossed the Rocky Mountains, then pushed north and east to the endless plains of Kansas. There they met a party of buffalo hunters who had heard no tales of golden cities. Nevertheless, Coronado continued on, finally reaching Quivira, a collection of poor mud huts "shaped like beehives," probably near present-day Salina, Kansas. It was time to go home. On April Fool's Day, Coronado and his men turned their backs on their golden dreams. In the fall of 1542, Coronado led the ragtag remnants of his army

Coronado and his men were disappointed when they reached settlements that were supposedly the Cities of Gold. They were greeted by the sight of poor, mud-brick dwellings—not an ounce of gold to be found!

The wealthy Spanish amassed many riches in the form of gold, such as gold coins and artifacts.

into Mexico. The failure had left him broken and disenchanted. He died ten years later, and with him faded the golden legend of the Seven Cities.

Other reports came from time to time, but no one believed them. Of course Cíbola was never found; it had never existed. Finally Cíbola faded to the land of vainglory's dreams, the land at the end of the rainbow.

Persepolis

May 330 B.C. A vast column of smoke and flame rises against the cobalt-blue night sky over the plains of Shiraz, in southern Iran. Persepolis, seat of the Achaemenid Empire and one of the grandest buildings of all time, is burning. Alexander the Great watches the sparks that whirl into the night. His mind is already on future conquests. Conquests that will take him, all in the space of 13 years, as far as India and Egypt, marching his army some 22,000 mi. (35,400km) to create an empire of more than 22 million sq. mi. (57 million km^2).

The ancient Persians called their capital Parsa, meaning "The City of the Persians." Construction began in 515 B.C. At that time, the Persian Achaemenid Empire spanned three continents, covering an area the size of the U.S.

Darius the Great, third king of the Achaemenid dynasty, decided that a grand palace should be built, an earthly version of the mythical City of Heaven, to serve as a religious and ceremonial center for the empire. He ordered a great terrace to be partially sculpted out of the Kuh-e Rahmet mountain and partially built on the plain. Continued by Darius's son Xerxes and by his successor, Cyrus the Great, Parsa was still unfinished when it was destroyed by Alexander.

Visitors to Parsa arrived by a wide ceremonial stairway leading up to the Gate of All Nations. Flanked by two great bulls 18 ft. (5.5m) high and made of polished black stone with their horns and hooves covered in gold leaf, two massive, gold-adorned wooden doors opened on to a reception hall. Emerging from the hall by the southern doorway between two statues of winged bulls with human faces, the visitors found themselves before the great palace, the Apadana.

A bust of a young prince from the Achaemenid dynasty. The artifact was found in the ruins of Persepolis.

On three sides, staircases lined with bas-reliefs led up to vast porticos. Each portico was held up by 12 columns, their capitals sculpted in the likeness of double-headed bulls. Huge doors 50 ft. (15m) high, covered in gold and silver, led from the porticos to the main hall—a forest of columns 6 ft. (2m) thick and 60 ft. (18m) high, with capitals in the shape of bulls holding aloft the enormous beams of cedar and cypress that supported the roof. The hall was large enough to hold no fewer than 10,000 people. Finally, the visitors arrived before the Throne of the King of Kings, the culmination of a visit they were unlikely ever to forget.

In 336 B.C., Philip of Macedonia declared war on Persia. Three years later, his son, Alexander, defeated the Persian army at the Battle of Issus, in Anatolia. After conquering Babylon, Alexander stormed the Persian gates and captured Persepolis. It burned to the ground in the days following, and the last of the Achaemenid kings, Darius III, was killed. The Achaemenid Empire had come to an end.

On March 21 (the first day of spring), delegations arrived from every nation of the empire, bearing gifts for the king. They are represented in bas-relief on the staircases of the Apadana. The carvings are so precise that they constitute a detailed catalog of the fashions of the myriad peoples of the Persian Achaemenid Empire.

Proud, golden-garbed Tecuciztecatl is reluctant to leap upon the pyre and become the fifth sun of the Dawn of the New World. Humbly dressed in paper and reeds, lowly Nanahuatizin does not hesitate—he jumps into the flames and becomes the sun god. The gods Eagle and Jaguar look on.

Teotihuacán

The ruins of Teotihuacán (pronounced "Tay-o-tee-wah-can") in central Mexico cover an area of 8 sq. mi. (20km²). Once the most important city in Mesoamerica, home to some 200,000 people, it was already ancient when the Aztecs discovered it around A.D. 1320 and coined its name, which means City of the Gods or "place of those who became gods."

Teotihuacán was a residential city and an important political and religious center for the surrounding area. The city was founded around 200 B.C. and reached its zenith about A.D. 500, but it was destroyed by fire around A.D. 750, probably by Toltec invaders.

The city was laid out in a grid pattern, with two main avenues, one running east to west, the other (the Avenue of the Dead) running north to south. The Ciudadela (Citadel) ceremonial compound is situated at the central point, where these two avenues cross. This is the symbolic center of the universe—the point at which, it is said, the world of spirit meets the natural world.

Teotihuacán is dominated by three stepped pyramids—the Pyramid of the Sun, the Pyramid of the Moon, and the Temple of Quetzalcoatl, which are linked by the Avenue of the Dead. Under the Pyramid of the Sun is a sacred cave. It is likely the Aztecs believed that here the first human beings of our era emerged from the underworld. The cave was formed naturally by flowing lava more than a million years ago, and on days of ritual importance, the setting sun shone directly into the cave's mouth.

Most of what we think we know about Teotihuacán is based on Aztec beliefs. For the Aztecs, it was a place of pilgrimage rather than a city in which to live. They believed it was at Teotihuacán that the gods gathered to recreate the sun and the moon at the dawn of the fifth sun—a time of a new cycle of creation. We live in the era of the fifth sun.

Mohenjo-Daro

The Indus river flows 2,000 mi. (3,219km), from a source in the Himalaya Mountains to the Indian Ocean, near present-day Thatta, Pakistan. More than 5,000 years ago, a Bronze Age people built cities on its banks. They called themselves "The Civilized," and their main centers, Harappa and Mohenjo-Daro, were built of brick and planned like today's cities on a square grid. In 1700 B.C., they were abandoned and lay buried until the 1920s, when the modern world rediscovered them. We now know them as the Indus Valley or Harappan civilization.

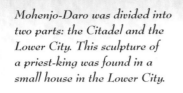

Mohenjo-Daro was divided into two parts: the Citadel and the Lower City. This sculpture of a priest-king was found in a small house in the Lower City.

In April 1847, Charles Masson deserted the British army in Agra, India, and struck out westward. He tells of seeing "in Harappa a ruined brick castle with walls and towers, built on a hill." Local legends described an ancient city and a curse attached to the hill, but the place was also used as a quarry of ready-made, hard-baked bricks, which were used by the local villagers for houses and walls. In 1857, British engineers took well-made bricks from a couple of nearby ancient cities for laying the railroad. All in all, 90 mi. (150km) of railroad between Karachi and Lahore are built on bricks 5,000 years old.

In 1919, an even larger site, called Mohenjo-Daro, was discovered. It was soon realized that this metropolis had been built by the same culture as that of Harappa. In 1924, the discovery of a forgotten civilization that had been lost for 3,500 years was announced to the world.

Mohenjo-Daro means "Mound of the Dead" in Sindhi (we do not know what the original inhabitants called it). It is the largest of the Indus Valley sites, which number more than 1,000. The city was built around 2600 B.C., but it was destroyed, possibly by repeated flooding of the Indus River, and rebuilt seven times before finally being abandoned 900 years later.

The city was a perfect grid system—a broad boulevard crossed from north to south, intersected at right angles by smaller streets from east to west. Mohenjo-Daro had one of the world's first sewers, with waste water flowing out of the city through covered drains. Houses were up to two stories high, with brick stairs up to flat roofs, and many had a bathroom and a well. They were not that different from those in the older quarters of Eastern cities today.

Archaeologists estimate that the city might once have had 35,000 inhabitants. But what do we know of them? The Harrappans could write, and they had a very precise system of measures, both for weight and for distances. Their bronze tools and weapons were elegant and functional, and they practiced dentistry and simple surgery. Necklaces and earrings of gold, agate, and carnelian have been found, as well as jars for cosmetics, but we have no names for any of the millions of individuals who created this vanished civilization.

Curiously there is little archaeological evidence of warfare or great kings. Mohenjo-Daro had no defensive walls, although it possessed towers to the west side and fortifications to the south.

Many craftsmen's workshops have been discovered—for metalworking, shell carving, and bead making—as well as potter's kilns and vats for dyeing cloth.

The theory that the inhabitants met a violent end at the hands of invaders has since been largely discounted. Most researchers agree that the Indus River may have shifted course, possibly because of earthquakes, and left the city without water. With wells drying up, crops failing, and river transportation no longer possible, it may well be that after a few generations the city was simply abandoned.

Perhaps the most vivid link to this vanished people to have emerged from the dusty excavations of Mohenjo-Daro is the discovery of hundreds of children's toys. Somehow, knowing that the people of Mohenjo-Daro had a flourishing toy-making industry makes them seem much closer to us.

Carts with oxen, animals with waggling heads, and pull-toy creatures with wheels were all exquisitely crafted from baked clay and stone.

This colorful vase decorated with an illustration of an ibex was found in the ruins of Mohenjo-Daro.

Shambhala

In April 1624, António de Andrade went north from Calicut, India. He was already far from his Portuguese birthplace, but he planned to walk to the roof of the world. The missionary had heard stories of Christians living in the earth's highest mountains, the Himalayas. His journey to find them sparked the beginning of a quest that is still going on today.

António de Andrade traveled as far as the border of Tibet, where he heard more tales of a mysterious mountainous realm, but snow and cold made him turn back. However, news of his trip spread through Tibet, and two more missionaries, Estêvão Cacella and João Cabral, were invited to visit. The king of Bhutan was delighted to meet the men and had a precious piece of information to tell them.

When the king helpfully explained that he had heard stories of a rich land to the northeast, called Xembala (Shambhala), he must have meant China. However, at that time the Tibetans did not know a great deal about the rest of Asia, and the missionaries, like many Europeans, would not have known any better. Cacella and Cabral did

not find Shambhala, but those few hints of a rich and unknown kingdom were enough to fire imaginations in the West.

The legend of a pure, mythical kingdom located high in the Himalayas is very ancient. In Sanskrit (the ancient written language of India), *Shambhala* means "place of peace or happiness."

The *Guidebook to Shambhala*, written in the mid-1700s, says the kingdom can be reached only partway on foot. The remainder of the journey is a spiritual one. Shambhala is mentioned in even earlier texts, notably from the Iron Age Zhang Zhung culture of Tibet and in the *Kalachakra Tantra*, one of the teachings of Buddha written around 400 B.C.

The fascinating possibility of a hidden kingdom in the vast Himalayas could only draw people to it, and naturally many set out to search for the lost land, but they have all returned empty-handed.

Rapa Nui

The statues, or *moai*, of Rapa Nui are immense and enigmatic effigies in human form. They are thought to represent chiefs or leaders of the past, erected to watch over the inhabitants and their villages. From the 1770s to the 1830s, during the war of *huri moai* or the "Toppling of the Statues," warring clans threw down their rivals' *moai*, pulling them forward on their faces. Boulders placed in their path broke the statues' necks on falling, destroying their power.

By 1840, not one statue remained standing. The quarries contain still more colossal statues, lying like giants in shallow graves. The largest measures just over 69 ft. (21m) and weighs 165 tons, twice the size of the biggest *moai* ever erected. Too huge to be moved, they were perhaps now-silent pleas for help to the gods themselves.

Lost in the midst of the vast South Pacific Ocean, Rapa Nui, also called Easter Island, is one of the most remote places in the world. The nearest land is 750 mi. (1,207km) north. South America is 3,000 mi. (4,828km) east, with Antarctica the same distance to the south. *Te Pito Te Henua*, the original name of Rapa Nui, means the "island at the end of the earth."

Around 2000 B.C., the peoples we now know as Polynesians left Asia and embarked on waves of colonization across the South Pacific Ocean. Settlers reached Rapa Nui in the seventh century. They found an island 63 sq. mi. (163km²) in area; it was covered in forest, with a wide variety of trees, some up to 100 ft. (30m) tall. Rapa Nui was home to busy colonies of both land and sea birds. Dolphins could be hunted in the deep sea waters, and nets were easily filled with fish. It was paradise.

When Europeans arrived on Rapa Nui in 1774, they found a barren land with sparse grass, poor plots of vegetables, and several jealously guarded chickens. The few thousand natives lived in flimsy huts and smoke-blackened caves. What had happened to the paradise island?

At its most populous, toward the mid-1500s, Rapa Nui was home to between 9,000 and 15,000 inhabitants. But the islanders had sown the seeds of their own destruction. The forests were felled, erosion carried away the soil, and even the climate changed. Streams dried up and drinking water became scarce. The birds were gone, nesting only on outlying islets. Fish were rare, and the dolphins had disappeared. This happened over many generations, perhaps so slowly that the islanders were largely unaware of the irreparable damage to their environment.

There are 887 moai and 125 ahu (platforms) on Rapa Nui; the longest ahu measures 656 ft. (200m). Some moai are coiffed by topknots of red stone thought to represent feathered headdresses.

This is a carved ancestral figure from Rapa Nui. The owner wore it at dances and feasts in hopes that the gods would grant the owner's wishes.

Dwindling food resources meant tension and strife. Warrior chiefs, called *matato'a*, rebelled against the royal families. For a generation, wars raged across the island. The population dwindled to approximately 3,000 people. But worse was to come.

The matato'a *devised a new religion—the cult of the birdman. This petroglyph (rock carving) from Rapa Nui shows a birdman wearing a bird's head and beak. The birdman was an islander who had control over the land's resources.*

A succession of whaling ships visited the island from time to time. The sailors brought diseases that often meant death for the islanders. Rapa Nui's darkest hour finally came between 1862 and 1880. Islanders were "blackbirded"—enslaved by unscrupulous merchants seeking to supply the demand for cheap labor in the guano mines of Peru. They unwittingly signed contracts they could not read, binding them to what amounted to forced labor, or they were simply kidnapped as slaves. Few returned; more than nine-tenths of the population perished or emigrated. When Chile annexed Rapa Nui on September 8, 1888, there were only 178 native inhabitants left. Today, the Rapanui represent two-thirds of the population of just over 3,000 inhabitants.

Every year, a swimmer from each clan braved the shark-infested waters in a race to a nearby islet where terns nested. The one who discovered the season's first-laid egg and returned with it intact was declared that year's birdman.

65

Uluru

Once upon a time, when there was no time, the earth was covered in salt water. The water was drawn away slowly north, and the sea has remained there ever since. The earth was bare and flat: the sun, moon, and stars had not yet come to rise in the sky. Slowly, the Eternal Ancestors awoke from their slumber beneath the earth and began to wander the land. They camped and hunted, lived and sang songs, and dreamed. Gradually, the land formed in their wake, each event leaving a landmark—a valley, a water hole, a mountain, or a rock of curious shape. Each landmark has a story. The stories of Dreamtime.

This map of Botany Bay was drawn by Englishman Captain James Cook (1728–1779). On April 29, 1770, Cook sailed his ship, the Endeavour, *into this bay. From 1788, European immigrants began to colonize Australia.*

The Rainbow Serpent laid eggs at a place where a rainbow hit the ground. These eggs turned into the distinctive rock shapes now known as Karlu Karlu.

This painting shows ten mimis—thin spirits that live in rock crevices. They are said to be able to reveal or seal the entrance to a cave just by speaking to it.

Near the end of the Dreamtime, when the land was almost complete, two tribes of snake-people, one poisonous, the other nonpoisonous, lived together near a water hole called Pugabuga. They were called the Liru and the Kunia. The Kunia grew restless and decided to move to the base of a huge, flat sandhill where there was abundant water. At the end of Dreamtime, the sandhill transformed into the rock called Uluru, and the Kunia became the boulders that surround its base.

Australia is a forbidding land—70 percent of it is desert or semiarid, with temperatures reaching over 120°F (50°C). Most of today's population lives near the coasts, and the outback is home only to sheep ranchers, opal hunters, and kangaroos. Nevertheless the Anangu (humans) thrived in the outback because they sang and dreamed the land. "Dreamtime" or "The Dreaming" is the framework of Anangu life. The true vision of the world can be found only in Dreamtime.

According to Aboriginal creation myths, the world used to be unformed and featureless. Then the Ancestral Totem Beings wandered Australia and formed the land by their dreams and actions. The original Spirit Ancestors, such as Honey Ant and Rainbow Serpent, awoke and rose from the ground and the waters and came down from the sky. They began to wander across the land. Like the Anangu who would follow them, they lived by making fires, digging for water, hunting, fighting, and performing ceremonies. Each of their actions left a trace on the land. Eventually, the whole land was crisscrossed by their wanderings and was complete. The Totem Beings changed into animals and stars or became features of the landscape itself. Reciting the story of these actions creates the songlines, which can cover a few miles or span the continent. Singing these events not only permanently re-creates the land but serves as a guide to water holes, food, and shelter. One songline can pass through many territories, each portion of it sung in a different tongue. In this way, by repeating and exchanging songlines in gatherings, the Anangu not only keep the land alive but can find their way through it without compasses or maps. Uluru is seen as the hub of the songlines.

The Rainbow Serpent arches above the land as the rainbow. During Dreamtime, he emerged from a water hole and traveled the continent, creating hills, waterways, and valleys.

Uluru is a spectacular outcrop of sandstone in the middle of Australia, and it is particularly beautiful at sunrise and sunset. The Sun Woman colors it with her bright rays each time she returns to sleep in her home in the west.

Timbuktu

With the unmapped portions of Earth rapidly diminishing as explorers sailed toward the poles, climbed the highest peaks, and trekked across every unexplored wilderness, the last frontier was to be found in the vastness of Africa. The coasts of the continent were well known, but the interior of the "Dark Continent" remained a mystery. One of these mysteries was the fabled city of Timbuktu, somewhere south of the Sahara Desert—the "sea of sand."

More than 100,000 manuscripts were kept by the noble families of Timbuktu, with some dating from as early as the 12th century.

The expression "from here to Timbuktu" means somewhere far away, somewhere so remote as to be the place where one never arrives. Less than two centuries ago, Timbuktu was indeed such a place. Then, in 1824, the Geographical Society in Paris, France, offered a prize to the first European who could reach Timbuktu and return to tell the tale.

But how could it be reached? To the north, east, and west, travelers had to cross the deadly Sahara Desert, with its wild tribes and ruthless brigands. To the south, there were jungles, with diseases, cannibals, and man-eating crocodiles.

And where was it? The name of Timbuktu comes from two words: *tin*, meaning "place," and *buqt*, meaning "distant"; *Tin-buqtu*, the faraway place. The city was known to be near the mighty Niger River, but the course of the Niger was still something of an enigma (it was fully mapped only in 1850). Getting there—and back—promised to be a dangerous, if not deadly, business.

For centuries, Timbuktu was a thriving metropolis, capital of the Kingdom of Mandingo, or Melli (Mali). It was an important trade stop between North and Central Africa, with boats and caravans carrying gold, ivory, slaves, cloth, ostrich feathers, hides, and, especially, salt. The city was also a center of religion and learning, and its most valuable treasures were books and manuscripts. During the rainy season, the countryside all around was green with forests, orchards, and crops.

The city reached its peak in the 15th and 16th centuries, with a population of around 100,000. By the end of the 16th century, however, trade had slowed, with ships landing at new ports along the coasts of Africa. By the 1820s, the Niger had shifted course, and the port of Timbuktu now lay 7 mi. (11km) from the city itself. The city said to be paved with gold was little more than a sprawling collection of huts.

To most people in medieval Europe, Timbuktu was a legend—an African El Dorado. As the mystery of the city remained, its reputed riches became all the more fabulous. The French Geographical Society reward was finally claimed by a daring Frenchman, René Caillié, who traveled for four long years from Sierra Leone to reach Timbuktu on April 20, 1828.

Timbuktu (Tenbuch) was shown for the first time on a map dated 1375, next to an image of the King of Mali wearing a golden crown and holding a gold nugget the size of an apple.

Caravans of camels carrying trade goods crossed the ferocious Sahara Desert to Timbuktu.

Timbuktu is now home to 30,000 people. It is a poor city, despite being a tourist attraction, and a UNESCO World Heritage site. The Timbuktu Manuscripts Project seeks to preserve the famous libraries. The buildings themselves, made of dried mud bricks, must be constantly repaired. But the legend is not dead. Timbuktu is still, in many ways, the faraway place at the edge of nowhere.

The Kingdom of Prester John

Venice, September 27, 1177. Pope Alexander III is writing a letter. It begins, "To his dearest son in Christ, John, illustrious and magnificent King of the Indians . . ." It is addressed to Prester John, priest-king of a mysterious and powerful Christian kingdom believed to be in the fabled steppes of Central Asia. The pope confided the letter to his personal physician, Magister Philippus, who dutifully set out eastward to deliver it. He was never heard from again.

Who was this king, so formidable that the pope would write to him personally? For several centuries, the kingdoms of Europe would dream and hope in vain of locating this lost Asian realm, before the dream finally faded four centuries later on the high plateaus of Abyssinia.

It all started with a letter. In 1165, a mysterious parchment circulated throughout Europe. It began, "I Johannes the Presbyter, Lord of Lords, am superior in virtue, riches, and power to all who walk under heaven. Seventy-two kings pay tribute to us. Our might prevails in the three Indies, and our lands extend all the way to the farthest Indies where the body of Saint Thomas the Apostle lies." The letter went on to list the marvels of the kingdom of Prester John. If only one-tenth was true, then it was certainly a land of marvels.

In the Middle Ages, the world was vast and largely uncharted. The interior of Africa was a land of legends, and giraffes and elephants were considered no less fabulous than unicorns and dragons. The idea of a lost Christian kingdom was certainly plausible.

This 1563 map of the Mediterranean shows Prester John (top) with the kings of Africa.

Venetian explorer Marco Polo reported in the 13th century that Prester John lived in Asia but had died in battle around 1195. Prester John is pictured here on a white horse in the book Travels of Marco Polo.

A century and a half after the last news of Prester John was heard, some Portuguese explorers finally found him —but not in Asia. In 1519, the Portuguese found a Christian king in Abyssinia, but his plates were not gold, as the fable told, and his name was Lebna Dengel. The dream faded back into the realm of legend, another earthly paradise long dreamed of, but never to be found.

Who wrote the famous letter, though, since Prester John never existed? Historians have been hotly debating this point for generations, and it is not likely that we will ever know. Prester John's letter became a sort of medieval bestseller, with successive copyists not hesitating to embellish and add details as they pleased. Eventually the letter, the original long since lost, became a work of fantasy.

Camelot

The splintering crash of lance on shield and the clash of swords can often be heard from the high ramparts of Camelot. According to legend, knights come from all over Great Britain, and even from foreign lands across the sea, to the fabulous court of King Arthur, hoping to prove their valor and perhaps gain a seat at the famous Round Table.

If the Age of Chivalry has a home, it is in fabled and magical Camelot. The legends of King Arthur and his knights of the Round Table are some of the most famous tales in the world.

Camelot is first mentioned in Chrétien de Troyes's *Lancelot, the Knight of the Cart*, written in the late 12th century. Chrétien certainly had in mind a royal court like those he knew, an assembly of people who followed the regent on his continual tour of his lands rather than staying at a permanent site. The *Mabinogion*, a collection of early Welsh tales written down in the 11th century, gives Arthur several magnificent courts in different regions of his kingdom.

Camelot only became a splendid city in the later stories of Arthur. In the Arthurian romances (medieval tales about heroes of chivalry penned by a multitude of authors throughout the Middle Ages), Camelot slowly takes form. By the time the English author Thomas Malory wrote *La Morte d'Arthur* in the late 15th century, the city of Camelot stood on the banks of a river and jousts were held in the fields before the city, which was set in the midst of plains and forests. Malory set Camelot at Winchester, England, but his publisher claimed the ruins of Camelot could still be seen in Wales. Many French romances place Camelot at Carduel, an imaginary city. A dozen sites in England have been proposed for the legendary castle.

In Arthur's castle, the king and his knights sat at the Round Table. The chairs were all the same—not even Arthur had a grander chair than his knights. All who sat at the Round

Merlin the Enchanter is an enigmatic figure from Arthurian legend. He obtains Arthur's sword Excalibur from Nimue, the enchantress known as the Lady of the Lake.

In one story, the boy Arthur pulls Excalibur from a stone, revealing that he will become king.

78

This illustration shows King Arthur and his legendary knights of the Round Table.

Cambraie (Welsh Annals) goes on to add that Arthur was killed at the Battle of Camlann in A.D. 537. Some scholars believe that both texts may refer to a Briton war leader, fighting against the invading Anglo-Saxons. Other historians claim that Arthur never existed. It is a debate that will likely never be resolved.

The legends of King Arthur fell out of fashion in the 16th century, only to be rediscovered in the 19th century. Since then, their popularity has never faded, and the stories are retold over and over. Camelot is a dream city, with its place firmly on the map of our imagination and inspiration.

Table were equal, and none could quarrel over the best spot. There was one seat, however, in which it was dangerous to sit. Reserved by the wizard Merlin for the knight who would find the Holy Grail, it was fatal for anyone else to try to sit there. Galahad, the perfect knight (in some stories, Perceval), at last dared to sit in the Perilous Seat.

French poet Chrétien de Troyes wrote about the Grail between A.D. 1181 and 1191. In the 13th and 14th centuries, the Grail became part of many stories, each borrowing from and building on stories written before. No one knows what the Grail is; it is a cup, a chalice, a platter, a cauldron, and even a stone in one German tale.

Before Arthur became the legend of the Once and Future King, he may have been a real man. The scribe Nennius, who wrote his *History of the Britons* in the ninth century, lists 12 battles fought by Arthur. The ten-century *Annalles*

An illustration of King Arthur from a tale written around 1300.

Avalon

Morgan le Fay looks down at the face of King Arthur, peaceful at last. Slowly, the boat pulls away from the shore. The hooded rowers are silent, their oars dipping soundlessly into the water. Far away, through the mists, the isle of Avalon awaits.

Others claim Arthur went across the sea to the New World, where Merlin's grave was found by the first British settlers in North America.

The legends of King Arthur are some of the most loved and enduring in the Western world. The stories of Arthur's kingdom, of Merlin, of the Holy Grail and the knights who seek it, as well as hundreds of other tales, are the work of dozens of authors from the Dark Ages to the dawn of the Renaissance. In countless versions of the story, King Arthur is taken by his half sister, Morgan le Fay, to the magical isle of Avalon to be healed—and to return to this world one day. Some scholars place Avalon in Britanny, France, or believe it might be Saint Michael's Mount, in Cornwall, England.

Avalon was first mentioned in A.D. 1136 by Geoffrey of Monmouth. In his *The Life of Merlin* (A.D. 1150), Geoffrey speaks of Avalon as "the island of apples . . . To that place . . . we brought Arthur, hurt by wounds."

The origins of Avalon are lost in the mists of time. It is possibly Annwyn, the Celtic Otherworld, where the inhabitants of Faerie found refuge from the world of mankind. *Aval* is the Breton and Cornish word for apple (*afal* in Welsh), which is probably Geoffrey's source for his interpretation of the name.

In 1191, three monks at Glastonbury Abbey found a lead cross bearing Arthur's name on a tomb in the churchyard.

Avalon was a misty, faraway land of legend, but it was anchored suddenly on solid ground in 1191. The monks of Glastonbury Abbey in England made a spectacular announcement—they had discovered King Arthur's tomb! In a coffin made from an oak trunk, buried deep in the churchyard, three monks found two skeletons. One was of prodigious size, with the marks of many wounds on the bones. At its feet were the bones of a woman, with a plait of beautiful blond hair. One eager monk seized the plait, and it crumbled to dust.

Circa 1193–1199, the historian Gerald of Wales wrote: "In our own lifetime Arthur's body was discovered at Glastonbury, although the legends had always encouraged us to believe that there was something otherworldly about his ending, that he had resisted death and had been spirited away to some far-distant spot."

Glastonbury was a Celtic holy place before the first Christian church was built there in the 7th century. Modern research has confirmed that a deep hole was indeed dug in the churchyard, but all the relics have long since disappeared. Whatever the truth behind the tale, the histories of Glastonbury and Avalon became one.

So where is Avalon? Perhaps searching for it on a map makes no more sense than preferring the real King Arthur to the legend. Avalon is everywhere and nowhere, but above all in the realm of the imagination.

Morgan le Fay has many faces. The first Morgan may be the Morrígan, the Irish goddess of battle, who can appear as a raven.

Glastonbury Tor rises above flat swampy land. By the Middle Ages, the land had been drained for farming, but before that the tor may have resembled an island.

Faerie

A leprechaun's money is not to be trusted. Silver coins always return to him and gold becomes leaves or ashes.

Bogles and brownies, pucks and pixies, fays and fetches, leprechauns, nymphs, banshees, gnomes, hobgoblins, sprites, elves, imps, and trolls—fairies come in all shapes and sizes. Beautiful or horrible, helpful or mischievous, they are the inhabitants and guardians of lands of golden dreams and dark nightmares—the perilous and magical lands of Faerie.

The term *fairy tale* was invented by storyteller Madame d'Aulnois in 1698, but the lands of Faerie have been with us much longer than that. There are many of them all around us, each with its own name. The theme of hidden people living in the world of humans has been a part of myth, folklore, and legend for a long time. Some nights— on Halloween or on Midsummer Eve—fairies come into our world, but the glamour and magic they cast around them is as dangerous as it is alluring.

Fairies are often called the Old People, and they lived in the hills, woods, and ponds long before mankind arrived.

These fey folk are especially plentiful in Ireland. The Tuatha Dé Danaan were a powerful Faerie people who arrived in the area from the north aboard a storm cloud. After a time, the Tuatha retreated to the islands of Tir na n-Og or placed powerful spells over their palaces to make them invisible, hiding them from mortal eyes with strong Otherworld magic. The Sidhe (pronounced "shee") might be found on islands and hills or in forests, rivers, and lakes. A grand castle, or even a humble cottage, may appear at night but be gone in the morning.

Time passes differently in Faerie. A night spent dancing with fairies may be a year—or many years—in our world. Humans are not always welcome in Faerie. Entering a fairy mushroom ring can be perilous, and accepting an invitation through a secret door or climbing onto the back of a strange horse can mean falling under a fatal spell.

Today, fairies live on in stories, and a tooth fairy comes at night to take a baby tooth placed under a child's pillow, leaving money in exchange.

A mushroom fairy ring is really a ballroom for dancing sprites and prancing hobgoblins. A grassy green hill has a secret door that we cannot see. It is visible only by the light of the enchanted moon, and it is dangerous to venture inside.

Hollow Earth

The idea of a hollow Earth remained the stuff of myth until, in the 19th century, the spirit of scientific speculation seized the idea. People had crisscrossed the globe with tracks and mapped much of it, but what did Earth's depths conceal? What lay in the center?

Dr. Edmond Halley (1656–1742) believed that "beneath the crust of the Earth . . . is a hollow void." He said the aurora borealis (the northern lights) consisted of a luminous gas escaping from inside the planet.

After a frozen mammoth was discovered in 1846, Marshall Gardner claimed that it had walked through the hole at the North Pole and frozen solid—proof that mammoths lived inside a hollow Earth.

In 1818, Captain John Cleves Symmes (1742–1829) published this claim: "To all the world—I declare the Earth is hollow and habitable within; containing a number of solid concentric spheres, one within the other, and that it is open at the poles . . . I pledge my life in support of this truth, and am ready to explore the hollow . . ." Symmes proposed uniting "100 brave companions" for a polar expedition to prove his theory. He thought that a person on foot would not notice his gradual progress over the rounded lip of the hole until he was inside Earth. Alas for Symmes, his ambitions attracted more mockery than money.

Soon thereafter, a New York doctor, Cyrus Read Teed (1839–1908), proclaimed that Earth was indeed hollow and that people lived not on the surface of the planet, but inside! In the center was the sun, which was half-dark and half-light, looking like sunset and sunrise as it turned. Only the dense atmosphere inside prevented people from looking up and seeing the other side of the world.

Hollow Earth became a destination of choice for writers of fantasy and science fiction, such as Jules Verne, who wrote the novel *Journey to the Center of the Earth*. From myth, with a brief detour into the realm of scientific speculation, the theory finally returned to myth.

Appendix of Lost Worlds

Here lie more lost worlds, hidden in the past, under the sea, in deserts or high mountains, or in the pages of legend.

Agharti
Deep under the Himalaya Mountains lies the legendary kingdom of Agharti, from where wise men and divine warriors will one day emerge to save the world.

Secret tunnels, known only by a select few, lead to the vast realm of Agharti.

Angkor Wat
Built in the early 12th century, the temple city of Angkor Wat in present-day Cambodia was the capital city of the Khmer kingdom.

Aratta
According to Sumerian legend, Aratta was a land of gold and riches, far away and hard to reach.

Carthage
This ancient city was founded by the Phoenicians in present-day Tunisia. The powerful Carthaginian navy ruled much of the Mediterranean until 146 B.C.

Cerveteri
The necropolis of Cerveteri, Italy, contains more than 1,000 tombs built by the Etruscans between the ninth and third centuries B.C. The origins of the Etruscans are lost in prehistoric times. They were conquered by the Romans.

Chichén Itzá
The sacred city of Chichén Itzá, Mexico, was the center of the Mayan Empire between A.D. 900 and 1200.

Delphi was one of the most important religious sanctuaries of the ancient Greek world.

Cockaigne

Tunnel through a haystack and emerge in a land of plenty, where pies grow on trees and you're never full. Such is the land of Cockaigne, a medieval legend from a time of famine.

Delphi

People came from all over the world to consult the enigmatic Oracle of Delphi on the slopes of Mount Parnassus, Greece.

El Dorado—legendary kingdom of gold

Each year, an Inca king coated himself in gold dust and washed in a lake, the bottom of which was said to be covered in gold. The Spanish conquistadors sent many doomed expeditions in search of El Dorado. It was never found.

Great Zimbabwe

Hundreds of curved stone walls and conical towers are all that remains of Great Zimbabwe, the capital of the Bantu civilization from the 11th to the 15th centuries. The ruins are some of the largest in southern Africa.

Hawaiki

According to Maori legend, 40 canoes left the land of Hawaiki and sailed to New Zealand. Spirits are said to return to Hawaiki after death.

Hy-Brazil

One day every seven years, the phantom island of Hy-Brazil can be glimpsed through the mist. However, it can never be reached, except in myth and story.

Kunlun Mountain

Somewhere in the Kunlun mountain range is the home of the Jade Emperor Yu-Hang, ruler of the gods and goddesses of heaven.

Lake Titicaca/Tiahuanaco

Where else but in the highest lake in the world would the Inca sun god Viracocha live? Lake Titicaca is found high in the Andes, between Bolivia and Peru.

Lemuria, or Mu

The lost continent of Lemuria, or Mu, in the Pacific Ocean, is considered to be the long-lost cradle of all civilization. Like Atlantis, it was destroyed by a cataclysm.

Ling

Legendary King Gesar was the fearless ruler of the ancient Tibetan kingdom of Ling. The "Epic of King Gesar," composed a thousand years ago, is still sung today.

Machu Picchu

High on an Andean ridge in Peru, the Inca city of Macchu Picchu was built around A.D. 1460 as a center for Inca rulers and abandoned 100 years later when their kingdom was destroyed by Spanish gold seekers.

Mag Mell

Mag Mell, the kingdom under the waves, is a land of plenty reserved for the dead. It is ruled by the Formorians, a race of giants that once inhabited Ireland. Like Tir na n-Og, it belongs to the Otherworld of Faerie.

Mesa Verde

The Anasazi built stone cities, or pueblos, and cultivated crops. The most famous of their cliff dwellings is at Mesa Verde, built under the overhanging arch of a great canyon wall in southern Colorado.

Mount Meru

Mount Meru is at the center of the Hindu universe and is the home of the gods.

Norumbega

Early maps of North America feature a land called Norumbega, in the vicinity of today's New England. Early explorers claimed the land was ruled by a tall and handsome people who worshiped the sun.

Saguenay

The Algonquin tribes told French explorers of a kingdom called Saguenay, ruled by a blond-haired people. The French eagerly searched for it, but in vain. It may be simply a myth, but it may refer to Viking settlements in Vinland.

Sheba

According to the Bible, when Solomon was king of Israel, he was visited by Balqis, the Queen of Sheba. No one is certain where the kingdom may have been.

Tartessos

The Bronze Age civilization of Tartessos, a harbor city in southern Spain, disappeared in the sixth century B.C. The site of Tartessos was discovered in 1958.

Thuvaraiyam Pathi

Described in Ayyavazhi mythology as a sunken island city more than 125 mi. (200km) off the coast of southern India, Thuvaraiyam Pathi is said to be where the human race began.

Mount Meru is said to be so high that the sun goes around it.

Tir na n-Og

There is no sickness or death on the Otherworld island of Tir na n-Og, the Land of Eternal Youth, somewhere beyond the horizon west of Ireland. Like Mag Mell or Hy-Brazil, it is hard to reach, and those who find it do not return.

Trapalanda

Trapalanda is a mythical South American city said to have been founded by shipwrecked sailors. Rumored to be a city paved with gold, set between two mountains—one of gold, the other of diamond—it has never been found.

Ubar

Ubar, or the City of a Thousand Pillars, is hidden in a cruel desert—the Rub al-Khali or "Empty Quarter" of the Arabian peninsula. Inhabited from 3000 B.C. to the A.D. first century, it was thought to be a haunted city of tall tales.

Uhlanga

According to Zulu mythology, Uhlanga is the marsh where humanity was created by the god Unkulunkulu.

Ur

Ur is one of the oldest cities in Mesopotamia. Capital of the Sumerian kingdom, it was built in the fourth millennium B.C. and finally abandoned in the A.D. fourth century.

Vaino-land/Northlands

According to the myths of the *Kalevala*, the Finnish national epic, Vaino-land is a northern land of deep forests and dark lakes, not unlike Finland itself.

After difficult relations with the natives (the Vikings called them Skraelings) the Vinland settlement was abandoned.

Vinland

In the A.D. tenth century, it is said, the Vikings discovered America when Leif Eriksson landed at l'Anse aux Meadows in present-day Newfoundland and called the area Vinland.

Xipangu

According to the explorer Marco Polo, Xipangu was a rich island kingdom to the east of Cathay.

Yonaguni

Mysterious underwater structures discovered in the 1980s surrounding the Japanese island of Yonaguni in the East China Sea have given rise to speculation about a lost civilization destroyed by an earthquake 2,000 years ago. Some scholars claim the structures are natural.

Ys

The magical city of Ys was built by King Gradon of Cornwall for his daughter Dahut. A great bronze wall protected it from the tides, but one night Dahut opened the city gate and a mountain of water submerged Ys forever beneath the sea.

Glossary

Age of Discovery
The period in history from the 15th to the 17th centuries when Europeans set sail for the New World.

agora
A marketplace in ancient Greece.

cataclysm
A devastating event, such as a flood, that causes great destruction.

cherubim
The winged guardians of the Garden of Eden and the Tree of Life.

chivalry
The customs and rules of knighthood.

Dark Ages
The time in Europe after the fall of the Roman Empire, from about A.D. 500 to 1000.

effigy
The likeness of a person or god, usually in the form of a sculpture.

erosion
A gradual wearing away of the land by the forces of nature.

irrigation
The supply of water to fields by means of pipes, streams, or channels dug into the ground.

Mesoamerica
Meaning "middle America" in Greek, Mesoamerica describes a culture and area that extends from central Mexico to Honduras and Nicaragua.

Mesopotamia
Meaning "land between the rivers" in Greek, Mesopotamia is the area along the Euphrates and Tigris rivers that today includes parts of Iraq, Syria, Turkey, and Iran.

necropolis
From the Greek for "city of the dead," a necropolis is a large cemetery, usually belonging to a city.

New World
The area that was new to Europeans in the 15th century, namely the Americas and Australasia. Europe, Asia, and Africa are called the Old World.

palisade
A strong fence made of stakes driven into the ground, forming the fortification of a settlement.

pilgrimage
A usually long journey to a place that is held sacred.

pillage
To rob someone of possessions, particularly during a time of war.

Pillars of Hercules
Two pieces of land at either side of the entrance to the Strait of Gibraltar, which connects the Atlantic Ocean to the Mediterranean Sea.

portico
A walkway or porch with a roof supported by columns, often leading to a building's entrance.

Renaissance
Meaning "rebirth" in French, this was an era of art, literature, architecture, and learning in Europe between the 14th and the 17th centuries.

Acknowledgments

First of all, thanks to managing editor Carron Brown and senior designer Jane Tassie, without both of whom there would quite simply have been no book at all. Special thanks to Neil Philip, whose painstaking research laid the foundations of many of the worlds, and whose equally painstaking proofreading and fact-checking kept me from going astray. Thanks to Christophe Dufour, of the Museum of Natural History of Neuchâtel, who graciously lent me a unicorn's horn. And, finally, thanks also to all those who helped with their special areas of interest: Gerry Embleton, Tamlyn Francis, Werner Froelich, Jean-Jacques and Diane Launier, William R. Iseminger, Bill Hollon, Shelley Noronha, and many others.

The publisher would like to thank the following for permission to reproduce their images (*t* = top, *b* = bottom, *c* = center, *r* = right, *l* = left): Pages: 7 "Gandalf the Grey" and "Rivendel" (detail) by John Howe are reproduced courtesy of HarperCollins Publishers; 8*tl* from *Forging Dragons* © 2008 Impact Books, an imprint of David & Charles Publishers; 8*tr* Digital Vision; 9*br* Digital Vision; 12*br* The Art Archive/Private Collection/Gianni Dagli Orti; 13*tl* The Art Archive/Bodleian Library, Oxford; 16*tr* and 16*l* akg-images/ Erich Lessing; 17 The Art Archive/Kunsthistorisches Museum, Vienna; 20*t* akg-images/Erich Lessing; 20*b* Werner Forman Archive/British Museum; 21*br* Werner Forman Archive; 24*b* akg-images; 25*br* akg-images/Erich Lessing; 28*tl* The Art Archive/Heraklion Museum/Gianni Dagli Orti; 28*bl* Corbis/Roger Wood; 28*br* The Art Archive/Bibliothèque des Arts Décoratifs, Paris/Gianni Dagli Orti; 29*tr* akg-images; 29*br* The Art Archive/Heraklion Museum/Gianni Dagli Orti; 32*l* The Bridgeman Art Libary/Bode Museum, Berlin, Germany; 32*r* The Art Archive/National Archaeological Museum, Athens/Gianni Dagli Orti; 33*tl* akg-images; 33*tc* Topfoto; 33*tr* akg-images; 35 (F7423) National Maritime Museum, Greenwich, London; 38*l* akg-images/Electa; 38*tr* The Bridgeman Art Library/Museo Archeologico Nazionale, Naples, Italy/Lauros/Giraudon; 38*br* Corbis/Sean Sexton Collection; 39*t* The Bridgeman Art Library/Private Collection/Accademia Italiana, London; 39*c* akg-images/Erich Lessing; 39*br* Corbis/Jim Zuckerman; 46*tl* and 46*tr* Cahokia Mound State Historic Site; 46*b* Corbis/Michael S. Lewis; 47*tl* Peter A. Bostrom/Lithic; 47*tr* Cahokia Mound State Historic Site; 50*l* Corbis/Sean Justice; 51*tr* Corbis/David Muench; 51*c* akg-images; 51*br* Corbis/Jeffrey L. Rotman; 51*b* Corbis/Jim Reed; 53*tr* The Art Archive/Archaeological Museum, Teheran/Gianni Dagli Orti; 53*bl* akg-images/Gerard Degeorge; 58*t* Corbis/Luca Tettoni; 58*b* Werner Forman Archive/Edgar Knobloch; 59*br* The Bridgeman Art Library/National Museum of Karachi, Karachi, Pakistan; 59*tr* Corbis; 64*l* South American Pictures/David Horwell; 64*r* Werner Forman Archive/British Museum; 65*tr* South American Pictures/Bill Leimbach; 68*tl* akg-images/British Library; 68*cr* akg-images/Henning Bock; 68*b* akg-images; 69*t* The Bridgeman Art Library/Private Collection/Dreamtime Gallery, London; 72*tl* Corbis/Wolfgang Kaehler; 72*bl* Corbis/Stapleton Collection; 73*tr* The British Library/HIP/Topfoto; 75*tr* The Bridgeman Art Library/Bibliothèque Nationale des Cartes et Plans, Paris, France, Archives Charmet; 75*c* The Bridgeman Art Library/Bibliotèque Municipale, Dijon, France; 75*b* TopFoto/The British Library/HIP; 75*br* iStock; 78*br* TopFoto/HIP/TopFoto.co.uk; 79*tl* The Art Archive/British Library; 79*tr* The Bridgeman Art Library/Biblioteca Nazionale, Turin, Italy, Roger-Viollet, Paris; 82*b* Lynne Newton, www.foxybiddy.com; 88*r* iStock; 89*br* Corbis/Jeffrey L. Rotman.